Nashua Public Library

Enjoy this book!

Please remember to return it on time
so that others may enjoy it too.

Manage your library account and
discover all we offer by visiting us
online at www.nashualibrary.org

Love your library? Tell a friend!

J

Invasive Species Takeover

CANE TOADS

BARBARA CILETTI

BLACK
RABBIT
BOOKS

Bolt is published by Black Rabbit Books
P.O. Box 3263, Mankato, Minnesota, 56002.
www.blackrabbitbooks.com
Copyright © 2017 Black Rabbit Books

Design and Production by Michael Sellner
Photo Research by Rhonda Milbrett

Library of Congress Control Number: 2015954691

HC ISBN: 978-1-68072-018-1   PB ISBN: 978-1-68072-282-6

Printed in the United States at CG Book Printers,
North Mankato, Minnesota, 56003. PO #1793 4/16

Web addresses included in this book were working and appropriate at the time of publication. The publisher is not responsible for broken or changed links.

Image Credits
Alamy: Ben Nottidge, 3, 10 (toad); Nature Picture Library, 4–5; Biosphoto: Daniel Heuclin, 19; Corbis: Joe McDonald, 24–25, 29; Papilio, 15 (left); Dreamstime: Alessandrozocc, 14 (eggs); Hupeng, 14 (tadpole); iStock: Click48, 20; dane-mo, 28 (top); Newscom: Emanuele Biggi/FLPA, 6; Shutterstock: Aleksey Stemmer, Cover, 8–9, 15 (right), 28; amorfati.art, 10 (map); Chris Ison, Back Cover, 1, 16–17 (bottom), 23, 31; Hypervision Creative, 32 (bottom); lantapix, 16,17 (silhouette); Phillip Holmes, 13; Steve Bower, 22; Superstock: Jean–Paul Ferrero/ardea.com/Pantheon, 7, 27
Every effort has been made to contact copyright holders for material reproduced in this book. Any omissions will be rectified in subsequent printings if notice is given to the publisher.

Contents

CHAPTER 1

A Deadly Toad

The city of Temple Terrace, Florida, had gotten a lot of rain. That rain was perfect weather for toads. A little dog, named Willie, was out in its yard. It came across a huge toad. Before its owners could stop it, Willie bit the toad.

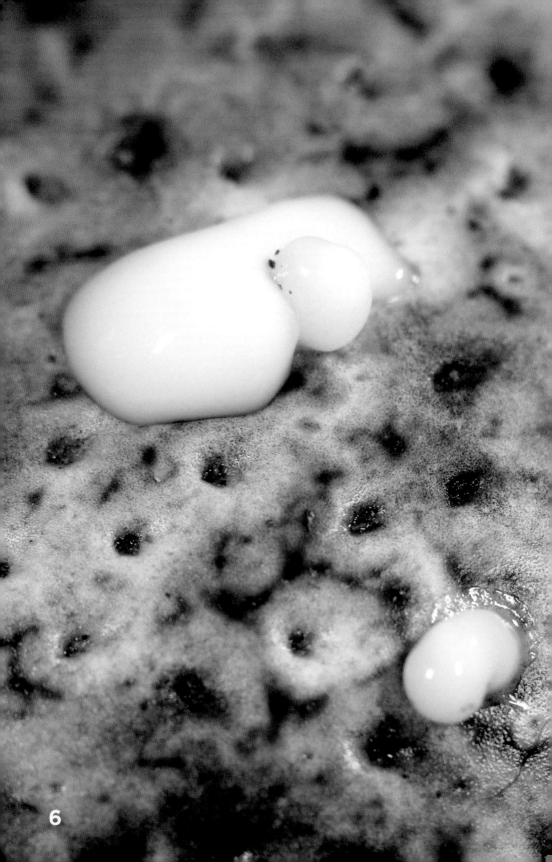

Poison Problems

Soon, the dog was shaking and very sick. The toad Willie bit was a cane toad. These toads are big and dangerous. They spray milky poison. And that poison can kill other animals.

GLAND THAT
HOLDS POISON

BUMPY SKIN

EYES

EYES

SNOUT

FEET

Australia

Invasive Species

Cane toads are not supposed to be in Florida. Years ago, people brought the toads to Florida. They easily spread throughout the state. They hurt the animals and plants that already lived there. Cane toads are an **invasive species**.

Failed Plan

Cane toads are a big problem in Australia too. People brought the toads there in the 1930s. They hoped the toads would eat beetles on sugarcane. The plan didn't work.

CHAPTER 2

Spreading Out

Cane toads are from South America and Central America. They live in warm forest areas near water. Cane toads were brought to the United States in 1955. Someone brought the toads through the Miami Airport. The person accidentally **released** the toads at the airport. The toads hopped away. They quickly made homes in Florida's **marshes**.

LIFE CYCLE of a Cane Toad

egg

tadpole

On the Move

The toads began laying eggs in their new homes. Females lay thousands of eggs at a time. The eggs hatch into tadpoles. In 34 to 50 days, the tadpoles grow into toads.

The new toads spread out, looking for food. They move to other water areas. And then they lay more eggs.

adult toad

young toad

cane toads' natural habitat

 where cane toads are invasive species

CHAPTER 3

Causing Trouble

Cane toads are trouble for other animals. They will eat almost anything. They eat bugs, lizards, and mice. They also eat pet food, garbage, and dead animals. Cane toads eat the food other animals need.

Cane toads are big **predators**. Scientists worry that the toads will kill **endangered** animals. They also worry the toads will harm **ecosystems**.

19

Poisonous Predators

Cane toads' poison is also dangerous. Animals that try to eat the toads get sick and die. People picking up the toads could have trouble too. The toads often spray poison when they are picked up. The poison can be very painful for people.

Pets can die from the poison in 15 minutes.

IS IT A CANE TOAD?

SOUTHERN TOAD

crests

oval glands

1.75 TO 4.5 INCHES
(4 to 11 centimeters)
LONG

CANE TOAD

large
triangular
glands····

no
crests

4 TO 6 INCHES
(10 to 15 centimeters)
LONG

CHAPTER 4

Stopping  Cane Toads

Scientists are looking for ways to stop cane toads. They are researching ways to stop the toads' **breeding**.

People can put up fences to keep toads out of yards. But fences won't stop the growing toad population.

Troubling Toads

Cane toads are troublemakers. But they do some good. The toads eat a lot of insects. They keep insect populations under control.

But their eating habits are also a problem. They could cause other animals to die out. That's why these invaders must be stopped.

CANE TOADS BY THE NUMBERS

.4 INCH (1 cm)

SIZE OF A BABY CANE TOAD

8,000 to 35,000

NUMBER OF EGGS A FEMALE CANE TOAD CAN LAY AT ONE TIME

5-10 YEARS

LIFE SPAN OF A CANE TOAD

5 pounds, 8 ounces
(2.5 kilograms)

WEIGHT OF BIGGEST CANE TOAD EVER FOUND

Think
about It. . .

1. What do you think should be done about cane toads? Use facts to support your answer.

2. Cane toads are a big problem in Australia. Use other sources to find out how the toads affect wildlife in Australia.

3. People brought the toads to the United States. Should people be allowed to bring animals to other countries? Explain why or why not.

GLOSSARY

breeding (BRED-ing)—the process by which young animals are produced by their parents

ecosystem (E-co-sys-tum)—a community of living things in one place

endangered (in-DAYN-jurd)—close to becoming extinct

gland (GLAND)—a body part that produces a substance to be used by the body or given off from it

invasive species (in-VAY-siv SPEE-seez)—animals or plants that spread through an area where they are not native, often causing problems for native plants and animals

marsh (MARSH)—an area of soft wetland that usually has grasses and cattails

predator (PRED-uh-tuhr)—an animal that eats other animals

release (re-LEES)—to allow a person or animal to leave a jail or cage

LEARN MORE

Collard, Sneed B. *Australia's Cane Toads: Overrun!.*
They Don't Belong: Tracking Invasive Species. New
York: Bearport Publishing, 2016.

Kallio, Jamie. *12 Things to Know about Invasive Species.*
Today's News. Mankato, MN: Peterson Pub. Co., 2015.

Somervill, Barbara A. *Cane Toad.* Animal Invaders.
Ann Arbor, MI: Cherry Lake Pub., 2008.

WEBSITES

Cane Toad
**animals.nationalgeographic.com/animals/
amphibians/cane-toad/**

Giant Toad
**www.wec.ufl.edu/extension/wildlife_info/
frogstoads/bufo_marinus.php**

Weird, True, and Freaky: Cane Toad Invades Australia
**videos.howstuffworks.com/animal-planet/35776-
weird-true-and-freaky-cane-toad-invades-australia-
video.htm**

INDEX